TIBET:
The Issue Is Independence

TIBET: THE ISSUE IS INDEPENDENCE
© All Rights Reserved, 1998
First Paperback Edition, 1998
ISBN 81-7621-028-5

By arrangement with Parallax Press, USA

Text design by Seventeenth Street Studios

Published by FULL CIRCLE
18-19, Dilshad Garden
G.T. Road, Delhi-110095
Tel: 2297792, 93, 94 Fax: 2282332

Printed at Nutech Photolithographers, Delhi-110095

PRINTED IN INDIA

*Dedicated to the Tibetan People
And in memory of Petra Kelly*

Contents

ACKNOWLEDGMENTS

Appreciation is due to the authors—
Lhasang Tsering, Jamyang Norbu,
Chukie Shakabpa Wangdu, Tashi
Rabgey, Yoden Thonden, Tashi-
Topgye Jamyangling and Bhuchung
K. Tsering; and special appreciation
to Professor Thubten Jigme Norbu
and his wife Kunyang and family
for their inspiration. Thanks are
due to Arnold Kotler, Ellen Peskin,
and Judy Hardin of Parallax Press,
publishers who care and are willing
to take a risk; Randall Goodall and
Lorrie Fink of Seventeenth Street
Studios; Galen Rowell, photographer;
Margaret Smetana, designer, who is
there for Tibet; and all those who
persist in their support of Tibet and
the Tibetan people.

THUBTEN JIGME NORBU

Introduction: Tibet's Independence

T HE TRAGEDY OF TIBET is at heart a man-made tragedy, one that has resulted from China's four-decade occupation of our formerly independent country. This occupation has brought death to over one million Tibetans through willful slaughter, and untold suffering to those who survived and have been subjected to bizarre social and economic experiments carried out by China in the name of "progress," a wretched process that essentially meant the Sinicization of Tibet.

The Chinese army marched into Tibet only a few years after the end of World War II, and a weary world seemed able to give no more than muted sympathy to the plight of Tibetans who found themselves deprived of the rights afforded them by the independence of their homeland. Tibetans have never wavered in their faith that one day the world will be moved to act in the face of what is plainly one of the great tragedies of the postwar world. Now over forty years later a great change has taken place as it has become increasingly obvious to people all over the world that the loss of Tibet's independence was only the first step in one of the bloodiest wars on a people and a culture in the postwar world. In recent years the question of Tibet has received greater and greater visibility. Finally, the just nature of the Tibetan quest for the restoration of Tibet's independence has started to receive the widespread and vocal support that it merits.

There are several facts that throw some light on the reasons for the refusal of Tibetans to submit to China's determined efforts to swallow up our country, including Tibet's history of independence from China up to the Chinese invasion of 1949 and the tragic situation that China created through its rule in Tibet. These should be reviewed briefly. It is sometimes stated, mistakenly, that Tibet, whatever its current legal position, has for a long time been at least a distant part of China. This is not at all the case. Most people don't realize it but Tibet first came into significant contact with China as a result of the rise of Tibet as one of the

great Asian empires in the early Middle Ages. Tibetan
armies fought and conquered territories belonging to or
contested by the empires of the Arabs, Turks and Chinese
in the period from the seventh to the ninth centuries.

During this time, Tibet itself was an occupying power
and ruled over wide stretches of land and territory in
Western China, at one point even occupying the Chinese
capital and forcing the Chinese emperor to flee. This great
martial strength collapsed in the ninth century, not because
of any setback on the battlefield, but because of internal
conflicts of the Tibetan court. This era of Tibetan conquest
was never repeated, perhaps because the period of the
Tibetan Empire was also the period in which the Buddhist
faith gained strength among the Tibetan people and ultimately became the major philosophical and ethical force in
their lives. In the centuries that followed one might justifi-
ably say that Tibet itself was conquered by Buddhism.

From the tenth to the thirteenth centuries Buddhist
ideas and philosophical schools of all sorts were continu-
ously transplanted from India into Tibet, where they flour-
ished. The effect was startling. When the Mongols rose to
power over Europe and Asia they were forcefully drawn to
Buddhism in the form in which it was present in Tibet.
Mongol reverence for Tibetan Buddhism has continued
into our own times, and even today the independent
Mongol state that has emerged from under Russian domination is reasserting its traditional faith.

While the Mongols dominated most of the Eurasian
land mass in the thirteenth and fourteenth centuries, it is
absolutely clear from all historical records that in their

domination they never made Tibet a part of China in any way, let alone an "integral part of China," as modern Chinese propagandists put it. The relationship between Tibet and the Mongol throne was wholly separate from that between China and the Mongol Empire. The Chinese argument that Tibet became a part of China under the Mongols is, on close examination, untenable. It is based on the reasoning that the Mongols were actually Chinese, and that China, as the homeland of the Mongols, was never subject to the Mongol conquest!

With the end of the Mongol Empire in China in the fourteenth century, Tibet and China resumed their places as independent neighboring states. All records, Chinese and Tibetan, clearly show that the Chinese emperors never inherited the power of the Mongols outside the borders of China. Only the subsequent Manchu conquerers of China were able to follow the pattern of the Mongols and to establish a large empire beyond the borders of China. This Manchu Empire endured from the seventeenth to twenti-eth centuries, and included China, Tibet, and Mongolia in its territories. But Tibet and Mongolia were never part of China, and when this empire collapsed in the early twenti-eth century both Tibet and Mongolia declared their inde-pendence.

Mongolia is still independent today, but the world turned its back when Tibet was subjected to Chinese aggression and swallowed up by the Peoples Republic of China. Even if one accepts Mongol and Manchu domina-tion as an historical fact, it nevertheless remains true that this domination was affected within the context of empire-building, i.e., as an aspect of imperialism. There is no small irony in the spectacle of "socialist" China asserting imperial rights to Tibet!

The differences between Tibetan civilization and Chinese civilization are vast. The Tibetan and Chinese languages are mutually incomprehensible and aside from a few borrowed words appear to be quite unrelated. Even the manner in which they are written differs with each language—the Chinese system incorporates thousands of different characters while Tibetan uses a thirty letter alphabet devised on an Indian model. Tibet, moreover, has been the home of a rich esoteric Buddhist tradition transmitted directly from India over a period of centuries. China received its Buddhism in a more compressed time period, and over the centuries Buddhism, one of several Chinese creeds, has often suffered stringent restrictions and persecutions. Even the Tibetan and Chinese canons of Buddhist scriptures vary considerably.

In addition to history, culture and religion, perhaps the most important point of all is that the Tibetan people themselves ardently desire independence from China. The will of the Tibetan people has been unambiguously expressed on a number of occasions, and it is fully on the side of independence for Tibet—the overwhelming majority of Tibetans understand that without independence they have no guarantees for their future. The core of the solution of the Tibetan issue is Tibet's independence. Until the time that Tibetans have full political control over their destinies, Tibet's future will be endangered. The determination of Tibetans in Tibet to attain their national rights as a member nation of the world community will not cease with any half-measure that puts their future in jeopardy. This should be obvious to anyone who has followed the course of political activity, protest and repression in Tibet during the last several years.

China has periodically followed policies designed to undermine the Tibetan identity and to rebuild it as a Chinese identity. The result of all this, however, has been to reinforce the determination of the Tibetan people to be free. I must emphasize that if Tibet is not accorded the right to choose independence, the Tibet question will never be settled. Anything less than independence for Tibet will simply be an agreement for further suffering, much as was the case of the Chinese 17-Point Agreement of 1951, which Tibet was forced to sign. Should the Tibetan Government-in-exile ever accept that Tibet is part of China, the Tibetan question will cease to be the concern of other countries. The creeping violation of any such agreement and the assimilation of Tibet into China (which is exactly what happened after the Tibetan government signed the 17-Point Agreement) may cause Tibetans to plead once more for their country, but what answer will they have when they are told that they willingly accepted incorporation into China? Incorporation into China will destroy Tibet's international identity.

This much is absolutely certain. The international response to recent cases of international aggression has shown us that only when a people's right to independence is clearly recognized by the international community can they hope for understanding, justice and assistance from the nations of the world. Even then, their hopes may remain unfulfilled. A people without that status will find themselves in even worse straits, as we Tibetans have seen from our own experience. Therefore it is absolutely essential that Tibet regain its rightful place as an independent state. Without that status the Tibetan people will lack the most basic tool with which to maintain themselves as free Tibetans in the future.

Any objective look at the international scene in the last few years shows that regaining Tibetan independence is now possible. At the same time we realize that there are a number of concerns that China may have that are legitimate; there need be no trouble in allowing China certain concessions in order to meet such legitimate concerns. But this can only be done on the basis of an equality of status between Tibet and China, on the basis of Tibet, like China, having an independent, internationally-recognized identity of its own. This is an absolute requirement for the safeguarding of the Tibetan future. China has said that aside from independence everything between Tibet and China is negotiable; Tibetans answer this by saying that with independence everything between Tibet and China is negotiable. We are willing to negotiate with China, but only as equals.

The essays that make up this volume address the concern for Tibetan independence from several perspectives. Nevertheless, all of the voices that the reader will encounter on these pages are ultimately expressing the common aspirations of the Tibetan people, both within Tibet and in exile.

The reader will also realize, in reading these essays, that serious contradictions exist between the majority of the Tibetan people and some politicians, both Tibetan and non-Tibetan. The majority of the Tibetan people realize that Tibet's independence is a wholly realistic desire at this point in history, when we have seen dictatorships of all sorts fail and suppressed peoples take their rightful place among the community of nations. Regrettably, some politicians have yet to understand that it is their conception of a monolithic China to which all must fully accommodate themselves—a China able to flaunt international norms of human rights without taking account of the desires of the people it is oppressing or the reaction of the international community—that is unrealistic and out of date.

It is a pleasure for me to present readers the essays that follow. I urge you to read them all, to consider the full significance of what they are saying; and, if you are convinced of the justice of the struggle for Tibet, to join us in working to restore to Tibet its rightful place in the world.

Thubten Jigme Norbu is the Director of the Tibetan Cultural Center in Bloomington, Indiana. Professor Norbu is the author of Tibet Is My Country *and* Tibet. *He was born in 1922 in the Tibetan province of Amdo. In 1950, Thubten Jigme Norbu was one of the first Tibetans to go into exile and to bring the Chinese invasion and occupation of Tibet to the attention of the world community.*

TASHI RABGEY

The Case for Rangzen

"To be silent in the face of great social evil is to be an accessory to injustice."
—Alexander Hescher

I AM OFTEN ASKED WHY YOUNG TIBETANS, particularly those in the West, continue to advocate independence. A generation has gone by since the unsuccessful uprising in 1959. In the intervening decades, China has only grown stronger and more formidable as an international presence. And those of us brought up in the West have presumably been exposed to the very best that the modern industrial culture has to offer. To the casual observer, the task of achieving an independent Tibet seems anachronistic, if not entirely absurd.

And yet the clarion call for *rangzen* (independence) persists. Indeed, it has become more adamant, more self-assured with the passage of time. For the independence of Tibet is about far more than the hollow euphoria of statehood, infinitely more than the false victory of tribalism. It is about justice and it is about moral responsibility. Most profoundly, it is about seeking to revolutionize the nature of relationships in modern human society.

Traditionally, the question of Tibetan independence has been discussed in the context of historical legitimacy. It is certainly not difficult to establish that Tibet was a single self-governing entity for most of its long history. This was due as much to the geopolitical realities of the region as to the efficacy of the central administration. Protected by a fortress consisting of some of the most insurmountable natural barriers on the planet, the Tibetan plateau was effectively isolated for over two millennia. Border scholars have thus characterized Tibet as the hub of the wheel in Central Asia—"nothing came across Tibet; everything went around it" ("Asian Frontiers," Alistair Lamb). Linked by ethos, customs and linguistic commonalties, the people of this vast, elevated plateau emerged as a distinct nation by the seventh century.

While the original pretext for the Chinese invasion in 1950 was to liberate Tibet from imperialist oppression—a rather odd undertaking given that there were less than a handful of foreigners in Tibet at the time—the Chinese

have since gone to great lengths to construct a convoluted
and at times bizarre historical rationale for the occupation
of Tibet. These fictitious claims are now being given very
little credence. Indeed, academics have given their
resounding recognition of the fact that Tibet had been an
independent state prior to 1950. This recognition, then,
serves as a meaningful point of departure for the discussion of the independence struggle itself.

What makes the case for rangzen truly compelling is the
collective modern experience of the Tibetan people. It is
now well-documented that the so-called peaceful libera-
tion was in truth an exercise in violent persecution and
senseless slaughter. The memory of the countless Tibetans
who have perished and the countless others who have suffered unspeakable anguish lives on, etched indelibly in our
minds. We cannot, and never will, forget the atrocities
inflicted upon our mothers, our fathers and the nameless
hundreds of thousands whose existence has been quietly
erased.

And yet, had the widespread persecution of the Tibetan
people simply been a product of isolated and temporary
ideological madness—as is now frequently contended—
current conditions would have to be assessed in a very different light.

Sadly, however, it has been made abundantly clear that
underlying the brutal atrocities committed by the Chinese
is a real sense of racist superiority. It is not surprising,
therefore, that even in an era of relative liberalism,
Tibetans continue to be marginalized and regarded as
being innately inferior. It is also not surprising that even

critics of the regime, such as reform economists Wang Xiaoqiang and Bai Nanfeng, reveal a condescending attitude towards Tibetans, openly referring to our "poor quality" as people. This conspicuous disregard for the entitlement of Tibetans to basic human dignity was succinctly demonstrated in a wall poster that appeared in Tiananmen prior to the massacre. The poster read simply: "Beijing is not Lhasa." It was understood to mean that recourse to violent repression is acceptable in Tibet, but not in the heart of the Chinese homeland.

Since even the dissidents of the Chinese society maintain a disparaging and contemptuous attitude towards Tibetans, it is painfully obvious that we are not being accorded the status and respect of full and equal individuals. Therefore, to accept their authority would be to accept the debasement of our own sense of self-worth. And thus to propose any political arrangement less than independence would be to expect Tibetans to accept their own self-destruction dressed in the blood-soaked garments of deceptive political jargon. It is for this reason that Tibetans have persisted in demanding the right to complete independence.

While the moral grounds for the legitimacy of the Tibetan struggle are self-evident, there is a further dimension which is too often overlooked: namely, the broader ramifications of the disappearance of the Tibetan culture. It is arguable that the Tibetan way of life could contribute significantly to the future as we enter a postindustrial age. This is not to say, however, that I espouse any inflated notion that Tibetans have been withholding some grand

secret from the rest of humanity or that Tibet should properly assume the position of the navel of the universe. On
the contrary, it would be a welcome development if the
popular image of Tibet as the utopian Shangri-la were defi-
nitely dispelled. Tibet was no utopia and injustice was far
from unknown.

However, every society, being an aggregate of fallible
human beings, will have its shortcomings. The question,
then, is one of degree. Despite its flaws, there is no doubt
that the culture which developed on the Tibetan plateau
was remarkably successful in meeting the needs and
desires of the vast majority of the people. This culture was
the product of a unique configuration of three factors: a
philosophical system which was concerned primarily with
the functioning of the mind, a harsh environment which
taught an appreciation for the limitation of resources, and
a virtual isolation which was both geographically defined
and, to an extent, self-imposed.

The Tibetan worldview, it seems, was derived primarily
from the Buddhist idea of the interdependent nature of all
phenomena. Tibetans thus understood the nature of reality
in terms of interconnected relationships. In practice, this
paradigm provided the insight necessary to accept the net-
work of responsibilities and obligations that was essential
for the creation of a fundamentally ethical society. The
fragile ecosystem of the plateau played a critical role in
reinforcing this understanding in daily life. Thus, a real
sense of individual responsibility was instilled in the people, both to each other and to the environment. Of course
this fundamental sense of moral and civic duty exists in

every human society. What sets Tibet apart from many others is that this ethos was allowed to take root and express itself to an extent which does not seem as evident elsewhere.

Why did it flourish in Tibet? Perhaps the answer lies in the fact that Tibet did not participate in the one phenomenon which has played the greatest role in defining modern human experience: mass industrialization. Irrespective of political orientation, this inexorable process has imposed upon all industrialized societies a linear model of progress. There has been in truth only one economic paradigm, that of perpetual growth and expansion. As the scale of the system has grown ever larger, a sense of alienation at the individual level has become pervasive. And this in turn has led to a virtual abdication of moral responsibility in vast segments of the industrialized society.

There is, however, growing recognition that we may be approaching the threshold to a postindustrial age. This is evident, for instance, in the marked shift in the nature of political discourse. State leaders are beginning to use the language traditionally reserved for organized violence in the context of environmental change. We now hear of "environmental security," the "green dividend" and "strategic environmental initiatives." Furthermore, as the linkages between environmental degradation and acute conflict in developing regions become more apparent, all levels of the global community will be forced to reexamine priorities.

What is needed, however, is far more than short-term solutions designed to provide pragmatic answers. Rather, the very basis of our relations with each other and to our environment needs to be reconsidered. But this does not mean renouncing material progress altogether. On the con trary, decision-makers must seek to integrate technology into a society genuinely founded on humane principles.

The culture of Tibet, like that of all human communities, was far from perfect. But it worked, for the environment as well as for the people. The profound grasp of impermanence shared by most Tibetans created a largely tolerant and inclusive society. Materialism was consciously eschewed for the sake of spiritualism. And if there was a single common doctrine in Tibet, then that doctrine was compassion. Its mantra—Om mani padme hum—was carved into the mountains and chanted with conviction into the winds.

We Tibetans now face the most critical period of our history as a people. In the last generation, the fabric of our society has been devastated. Chinese settlers now out-number Tibetans in Tibet, while in exile, we have in so many respects absorbed the norms and mores of our adopted homes. Sadly, it is doubtful whether efforts to pre-serve the culture in exile will manage to capture the true essence of the Tibetan way of life. For the spirit of Tibet is inextricably tied to the enduring solitude of the wind-swept plateau. This spirit yet lives within the people of Tibet— but they have long been covered by the darkness of the night.

If we have learned one thing, then, it is that our very survival depends upon the achievement of a genuinely free

Tibet. The issue, therefore, is independence. Towards this end, our cries will be relentless and our cries will be heard. We will not be silent.

Tashi Rabgey was born in 1969 in Dalhousie, India. Before the age of two, she and her family moved to Canada, along with 285 other Tibetan refugees. In the mid-1970s, her family began a Tibetan folk arts ensemble that exposed her to the richness of the Tibetan heritage at an early age. In 1987, she traveled to Tibet. She completed her bachelor's degree in economics and international relations at the University of Toronto. Currently she is reading law at Oxford University on a Rhodes Scholarship.

JAMYANG NORBU

The Heart of
the Matter

*"If one does not know to which port one
is sailing, no wind is favorable."*
—Seneca

T HE WORD "REALISTIC," whenever introduced into any
discussion on Tibetan politics, never fails to set my
teeth on edge. It invariably signals the opening of the
argument that if the Tibetans compromised on the
question of independence, and accepted some form of
autonomous status within China, then the Chinese authorities would reciprocate with concessions. Though not as

17

preferable as independence, this would make life inside Tibet more tolerable, and hence ensure the survival of the Tibetan people.

On the face of it, a reasonable argument. So what's the catch? Well, for one the Chinese have *never* evinced any desire to discuss a compromise solution—not even the most pathetically watered down one proffered by Dharamsala, the site of the Tibetan Government-in-exile. But certain Tibetan ministers, officials and some foreign friends will insist that there have been positive signals from the Chinese, at least on occasions, indicating their willingness to talk. So who's being untruthful here? No one, really—at least not willfully so.

Early this century astronomers worldwide saw through their telescopes intricate networks of canals radiating all over the surface of Mars. On the strength of this evidence the theory was put forward of a great Martian civilization that had once built this monumental system of waterways. There were two main causes for this mass delusion: one, everyone wanted to believe that there were canals, hence civilized life-forms on Mars; two, there was a linguistic misunderstanding. The astronomer who first made the discovery was an Italian, Giovanni Schiaparelli, who reported the sighting of "*canali*," which in Italian means channels, not man-made "canals."

Our delusion, which eventually fossilized into a full-fledged and official *idée fixe*, began with the introduction of Deng Xiaoping's Four Modernizations and the announcement of the first fact-finding delegation to Tibet in 1979. I recall the excitement and hopes these events generated in

Dharamsala at the time. Going back to Tibet suddenly
appeared to become an immediate possibility. There was
even a mild panic among building owners in McLeod Ganj
(the exile area in India). I went around deliberately pouring
cold water on these expectations, and did not particularly
endear myself to those who had most need to subscribe to
such fantasies, namely, the naive people in power.

Everyone talked of the Four Modernizations, but no
one, except for myself, seemed to have heard of the Four
Absolutes—which were essentially Deng's way of saying
that, aside from economic liberalization, he would tolerate
no criticism of, nor challenge to the Party's absolute power.
I am sure that, even now, many Tibetans and friends have
not heard of this disturbing obverse to the Four Modernizations. Furthermore, everyone at the time seemed to
assume that Deng Xiaoping was a fresh entrant on the
Communist political scene, like Gorbachev, and not that
he was one of the oldest Communist Party leaders, some-
one who even opposed Mao for initiating the Hundred
Flowers Campaign to allow some criticism of the Party.
Later, when Mao reversed his line, Deng was put in charge
of the anti-rightist campaign to take care of "stinking"
intellectuals and critics of the party. About 2.9 million people were accused of rightism. About 500,000 by Deng's
own estimate offered in 1980, were condemned. The campaign was marked by great brutality.

No great intellectual perspicacity was required to see
that the cause of Tibetan independence would soon
become a bargaining chip in our futile bid to elicit some
concession from China. I mentioned these misgivings in a

number of articles in the *Tibetan Review*, but like most things I wrote at the time, they had as much impact on actual events as a "fly beating its wings against a boulder," which was how Chinese authorities in Tibet, betraying an unexpected penchant for colorful imagery, disparaged my writings.

Whenever the Tibetan issue has received any substantial attention in the world, be it with the demonstrations in Lhasa, or the awarding of the Nobel Peace Prize to the Dalai Lama, the Chinese have mostly always succeeded in sidetracking international concern by making titillating press announcements the next day announcing how willing they were to sit down and talk with the Dalai Lama or his representatives. Those sympathetic to Tibet naturally heave a huge sigh of relief and the situation is effectively defused. At Dharamsala, a delegation to Beijing is announced, and fierce intrigues are conducted by various political factions to get their man on the team. It all comes to nothing, of course. Once in a while, though, the delegation does actually get to go to Beijing. They invariably return to Dharamsala in a daze, with a look on their faces not unlike that on Charlie Brown's when he is lying flat on his back, after having been persuaded by Lucy for the umpteenth time to take a running kick at a football that she never fails to yank away at the last moment. "Isn't trust a wonderful thing, Charlie Brown?"

Aside from Deng Xiaoping and Li Peng, another and equally unpleasant politician who has been successfully pulling off something like this has been the Bosnian Serb leader Radovan Karadzic. For the last two years, every time a U.S. president began to talk seriously of using force to halt the bloodshed in Bosnia, Karadzic has at once been cooing sweet reason, talking of getting all the warring parties to a conference, and whatnot—keeping up the patter long enough till Western resolve became deflated.

To be fair to Chinese leaders, it wasn't a lie, at least not an outright one, when they said that they would be willing to sit down and talk with Tibetans. Whenever Beijing declared its readiness to discuss "all other issues" if Tibetans gave up talk of independence, we never asked ourselves what exactly they meant by that wonderfully vague phrase. We always assumed that it would either be the question of autonomy, or some other special status within China—maybe even a variation on Michael van Walt's "associate status."

But if one carefully goes through all that the Chinese have actually said concerning dialogue with Dharamsala, there is absolutely nothing to indicate their willingness to make even the tiniest of concessions. So what do the Chinese really want to talk to Dharamsala about? I think they made that clear in the only statement they issued where they specifically mentioned what they were prepared to discuss. This statement was made by Hu Yaobang in 1984 and laid down five points for discussion; these essentially dealt with knotty details that would arise from the Dalai Lama's return to the "motherland"—after he had given up on independence: questions like his political rank (would he be restored to his vice-chairmanship in the National People's Congress?), whether he would be allowed to live in Lhasa or maintain a ménage in Beijing,

by what route he would make his journey and so on. That
is the furthest extent to which Beijing has been willing to
enter into any talks with Dharamsala. And that's all.
Everything else is strictly China's internal affairs, whether
it be the political status of Tibet, human rights, environmental issues, or the search for the reincarnation of the
Panchen Lama. It's nobody else's business, least of all,
Dharamsala's.

The main proponent of giving up independence and
cutting a deal with China is the Dalai Lama's brother,
Gyalo Thondup, who is a minister in the kashag (Tibetan
cabinet). He has been energetic in spreading the message
that Tibetans-in-exile should give up the hopeless cause of
independence and return to Tibet. He is not one of those
prophets conspicuous for leading by example. So far neither he nor any of his immediate family have shown any
inclination of abandoning their own relatively comfortable
lifestyles in exile to return to Tibet. But what G.T. (as he is
known to the less reverent) lacks in this respect he makes
up for in the intensity with which he has been conducting
his campaign. There has been a large demonstration by a
rent-a-crowd contingent of naive students from the school
for new arrivals, at Bir, especially trucked in to Dharamsala, most carrying placards and banners, some even
wearing headbands declaring "We love Gyalo."

Threats of violence and arson have been made to the
Tibetan Youth Congress who, in an issue of their maga-
zine, Rangzen, carried letters from Tibetans in North
America, Europe and Japan protesting against speeches
made by Gyalo Thondup when he visited North America

in 1992. In his talks G.T. had reprimanded Tibetans living in the U.S. and Canada for hurting the Chinese economy by organizing boycotts of Chinese goods, and campaigning against Most Favored Nation status for China. He voiced a personal concern that if China lost the MFN status it was possible that over 40,000 people could lose their jobs in Guangdong province alone. All of this was in addition to his usual message of the impossibility of achieving Tibetan independence and the need to cut a deal with the present leadership in China.

Through threats and intimidation an ugly climate of fear and suspicion has been created in Dharamsala where if one declares oneself for Tibetan independence there is every possibility of finding vicious accusations directed at oneself of being "against the Dalai Lama." One of the unfortunate consequences of all this has been the outbreak of large-scale fighting at the school for new arrivals from Tibet, at Bir, where pro- and anti-Gyalo Thondup factions, involving a few hundred students, battled it out with knives, rocks, sticks and axes. The school was effectively closed down for a number of months, adversely affecting the studies and lives of hundreds of innocent students from Tibet. The school has reopened only recently, but residual violence remains. The principal was assaulted violently by two students, just a month ago. The school had about 750 students before the outbreak of trouble, now it has about four hundred and fifty.

A writer friend of mine, a new arrival from Amdo, Pema Bhum, has been constantly harassed and threatened with violence, even murder, for allegedly "opposing the

Dharma" in an academic paper on modern Tibetan literature that he had presented at a Tibetology conference in
Italy last year. The real reason for his unpopularity with a
section of politicians here, has probably more to do with
his attempts to dissuade the students at the Bir school
from getting involved in Dharamsala factional politics. He
also offended many supporters of G.T. at a large meeting
of Amdowas (Tibetans from the Amdo region), where he
raised a sole dissenting voice when everyone there decided
to withdraw from the Tibetan democratic process, if the
parliamentary committee investigating G.T.'s controversial
statements was not called off.

Gyalo Thondup affects a somewhat olympian attitude
in matters of statecraft, coolly making public statements
absolutely contrary to Tibetan government policies—and
getting away with it too. A rather craven parliamentary
investigating committee cleared him on this matter, justify-
ing his controversial statements on the grounds that they
were only "personal opinions." There is more than a touch
of the late Chiang Kai-shek in G.T.'s political makeup,
which is not at all surprising seeing he was educated at a
Guomindang school in Nanjing just after World War II,
and was reputedly close to the Generalissimo's family.
Nothing sinister about that, of course. However, such an
influence, especially during one's formative years, is probably not conducive to the flowering of any democratic sen-
timents in one's later political development. G.T. likes to
operate only at the highest levels of polity, and claims to
be on close terms with Deng Xiaoping and other top
Chinese leaders. G.T. once lectured to me, in his slightly

Chinese-accented English, about how he had reproached Chinese leaders in Beijing for their heavy-handed tactics in Tibet.

I would probably once have been flattered by such a sharing of confidences, and impressed by this anecdotal, yet nevertheless heady, proximity to great people and events; but by then I had read of Chamberlain being "firm" with Hitler, while Göring and Ribbentrop were laughing in the anteroom. It is now a political rule of thumb with me that an accurate perspective on monsters can only be obtained at a distance. You get too close and all you see are rather ordinary people, asking only to be understood and admired. "The banality of evil" was, I believe, the phrase applied by Hannah Arendt to the revelations of the Eichmann trial in Jerusalem. Dictators, and hence politicians by extension, must be judged by their deeds, not by what they say or promise, nor by their "friendship" with one, no matter how close or seemingly genuine.

We have to be particularly wary of Chinese leaders. Over and above the usual set of treacherous vices that seem to be standard issue to modern despots, Chinese leaders are the inheritors of an ancient tradition of "barbarian control" that has been used with an impressive degree of success against Tibetan, Uigur, and Mongol *fan quan* (barbarian officials). Distinguished visitors from the west like John Kenneth Galbraith, Edward Heath, Richard Nixon, Margaret Thatcher, George Bush and others, have been courteously subjected to the same, and have all dutifully gone through their paces with the eager compliance of performing poodles.

In recent months, Gyalo Thondup has had talks with
Chinese leaders at Taipei, and more recently Beijing. In
view of his previous indiscretions, G.T. has been accompa-
nied by official "minders," two on his Taipei visit and one
for Beijing. The peculiar thing about this arrangement is
that none of the officials accompanying G.T. speak a word
of Chinese, and the negotiations have all been conducted
in that language. This has raised the suspicion among
many, including, I understand, the aides themselves, that
the participation of these three officials was nothing more
than window dressing for Tibetan public opinion, behind
which G.T., once again, did exactly as he pleased.

Like American Indian chiefs going to see the "Great
White father" in Washington, D.C., Tibetan politicians
have vied with each other to get a berth on delegations to
Beijing. Whether this "one-sided infatuation" *(dan xiang
si)*, as the Chinese so aptly put it, serves any national purpose is debatable, but it provides our politicians an illusion of playing on the big tables, and like most power
drugs of this kind, produces an irresistible addiction.

I think His Holiness now realizes how misplaced his
efforts to initiate a dialogue with the Chinese has been.
The first indication came on April 17, 1993, at the Institute
of Performing Arts in Dharamsala. After watching a Lhamo
performance, the Dalai Lama made an unexpected political statement in which he mentioned that all the many
efforts made by him and the Tibetan government to negotiate with the Chinese had made no headway. He also
expressed his fears that Chinese overtures concealed a
darkly insidious and long-term plan for ensuring the end of

Tibetans as a nation and people. He concluded that Tibet now faced its greatest danger in the ever increasing immigration of Chinese settlers. He called on all Tibetans and friends to do everything they could to fight this threat.

One of the latest arguments of the anti-independence lobby has been on this issue of Chinese immigration to Tibet. What is claimed is that the question of the survival of the Tibetan people is now so acute, that even the cause of independence must be sacrificed in order to ensure social survival. But where on earth is the connection? Have the leaders of China even hinted that if Tibetans gave up their claims to independence it would halt Chinese immigration? Of course not! Giving up the cause of a free Tibet and everyone in exile returning quietly to Tibet would ensure an even quicker end to the existence of the Tibetan people.

Anyhow, I mistrust this "sudden" discovery of the dangers of Chinese immigration. Right from the mid-eighties it was obvious to all but the most willfully stupid, what the Chinese were doing. I wrote a detailed two-part article on this subject six years ago in the *Tibetan Review*. Even earlier I knew of a number of concerned Tibetans who, after visiting Tibet, had warned the Tibetan government of the growing threat of Chinese immigration to Tibet. But some of the people who now claim to be desperately worried by Chinese immigration, are in fact the very people who were pooh-poohing reports of Chinese immigration six years ago, preferring then to believe that a wonderful deal with China was just around the corner.

For a number of years now the few Tibetans who have

vocally insisted on maintaining the cause of an independent Tibet have often been seen by non-Tibetan supporters
of Tibet as dangerous extremists, undermining the good
work of all those working towards the far nobler goals of
establishing Tibet as a zone of peace or a Buddhist environmental theme park, and promoting the Dalai Lama as a
global new-age guru.

"Nationalism" has always been a dirty word to those
Westerners who have been interested in Buddhism and
Tibet. And with the present murder and mayhem in the
Balkans and parts of the former Soviet Union, all let loose
by unbridled nationalistic passions, who can say that they
are entirely in the wrong? At the same time, I cannot but
help note that the critics of nationalism are invariably
those who have a *pukka* (internationally recognized) pass-
port, and a nation of their own to return to, when
Dharamsala or Lhasa may get too depressing or dangerous. The internationalist may find the idea of nation states
old-fashioned and limiting, but at the moment that's all
we've got (and some of us haven't got it). People who have
it can afford to speculate on alternatives, but they should
not, like Marie Antoinette, push their preferences on more
unfortunate people. Cake may be exciting, but bread sus-
tains life. Tibetans would like a loaf, please.

Some years ago, when my friend Lhasang Tsering and I
were giving a talk at the University of Calgary, a Chinese
student asked a question which I had previously encoun-
tered in the writings of certain experts on China (David
Bonavia) and Tibet (Mel Goldstein). The thrust of it was
that, yes, the Tibetan case for independence was not

entirely without cause or merit, but the reality of it was
that they would never get it. So why shouldn't they recon-
cile themselves to Chinese rule and attempt to benefit from
it? After all, even China, a former victim of Western imperialism, had benefited from that humiliating experience, in
the sense of being forced to learn about modernization
from its oppressors; as had other countries in Asia and
Africa.

Not only is such an outlook historically ill-informed on
the character of old style empires and imperialism, but it is
dangerously naive on the nature of modern totalitarian
nations, especially when the nation in question has the
chameleon ability to change everything about itself in
order to survive—everything except the permanent core of
lies and repression.

Churchill, in his *History of the English Speaking People*,
relates the fate of Britain as a Roman colony, after British
resistance had been overcome: "For nearly three hundred
years Britain, reconciled to the Roman system, enjoyed in
many respects the happiest, most comfortable, and most
enlightened times its inhabitants have ever had. In culture
and learning the land was a pale reflection of the Roman
scene, not so lively as the Gallic. But there was law; there
was peace; there was warmth; there was food; and a long-
established custom of life. The population was free from
barbarism without being sunk in sloth or luxury. Some culture spread even to the villages. Roman habits percolated;
the use of Roman utensils and even of Roman speech
steadily grew. The British thought of themselves as good
Romans as any.... There was a sense of pride in sharing in

so noble and widespread a system. To be a citizen of
Rome was to be a citizen of the world raised upon a
pedestal of unquestioned superiority above barbarians
and slaves."

The celebrated Indian writer Nirad C. Chaudhuri, dedicated his *Biography of an Unknown Indian* to the memory
of the British Empire, saying "all that was good and living
within us was made, shaped and quickened by the same
British rule."

But if Chaudhuri is too much the anglophile, let us take
the views of an Indian less enthusiastic about British rule.
Gandhi in his autobiography, *The Story of My Experiments
with Truth,* says, "Hardly ever have I known anybody to
cherish such loyalty as I did to the British Constitution. I
can see now that my love of truth was at the root of this
loyalty. It has never been possible for me to simulate loyalty or, for that matter any other virtue.... Not that I was
unaware of the defects in British rule, but I thought it was
on the whole acceptable. In those days I believed that
British rule was on the whole.beneficial to the ruled."

I am not trying to justify Roman or British, or any other
kind of imperialism here. Of course, Gandhi was right to
later change his mind and fight for independence.
Whatever benefits imperial rule may confer on its colonial
subjects, in the end it makes them lesser people. The costs
outweigh the benefits, and how much more so for those
under Chinese rule, where such benefits are nonexistent.

I do not think it necessary to go into detailed compar-
isons here, but let us take one of the most important foun-
dations of any society—law. Nearly all the legal systems of

present-day European nations are based, in one form or
another, on Roman law, on the *Codex Justiniani*, the
Emperor Justinian's great legal code. Transcending even its
legal function, Roman law, in the end, became one of the
greatest intellectual forces in the history of European civilization.

The British Empire's greatest legacy to India is constitu-
tional government and the concept of law. Imperfect as the
system is, it is still the lifeblood which powers the country's democracy, and the sinews with which its disparate
people are bound together as a nation. I think it can be
said without exaggeration that nothing remotely similar
has taken place in Tibet. Instead, the lessons we learned
from the Chinese, legal and otherwise, have not only been
negative, but pernicious in the extreme. Even now, with
the liberalization in the economy and social lifestyle, the
law in China is no more than just an instrument of state
repression.

Taking into account the constant lies, struggles, mutual
surveillance, denunciations, institutionalized violence,
leader worship, "Reform through Labor," and cultural revo-
lutions (of one sort or another) inflicted on the Tibetan
people for over four decades, it is surely a miracle that
they have not altogether regressed into hopeless depravity,
cynicism, drunkenness, brutality and madness. A triumph
of the Tibetan character? One would think so from reading
fairly recent accounts of "smiling friendly" natives in
recent travel books on Tibet. Complimentary certainly, but
not too discerning of the fearful bashing the Tibetan spirit
has taken. No psychological study has been conducted of

the people living inside Tibet, but I have the very uneasy feeling (I hope I'm wrong here) that the damage inflicted on the mental health of the Tibetan people far outweighs the destruction of the monasteries and temples.

In the final reckoning, I am convinced that Tibetans must have independence if only for survival as a people. With every passing year we are getting closer to extinction. Aside from the deliberate Chinese government policies to erase Tibetan identity by sending Tibetan children to schools in China, or making Tibet a special economic zone, the sheer relentless pressure of China's exploding population will eventually push Tibetans to extinction. No autonomy, or any kind of understanding or accommodation with China will prevent it. One cannot accommodate an avalanche, neither can one stop it halfway. Only full independence holds out some hope for Tibetan survival— even that is touch and go.

I am in no way claiming that achieving independence will be easy—or even possible, in the near future. All I am saying is that in the cold clear light of all the evidence that we have before us, the struggle for independence, no matter how desperately hopeless it may appear, holds out at least a better chance for Tibetan survival. The various fantasies being espoused in the name of compromise, understanding, and realism only serve to divide Tibetan society and provide legitimacy to all kinds of dubious self-styled experts, "honest" brokers, pocket Kissingers, "friends" of Chinese leaders, even well-meaning imbeciles—all eagerly contributing to the production of an effectively disorienting smoke screen of policy confusion (do the Tibetans want associate status, a zone of peace, human-rights, some help with the environment, freedom, a vatican for the Dalai Lama, or emigration to America; what do these people really want?), behind which the Chinese are going about the business of resolving the issue once and for all.

Jamyang Norbu was educated at St. Joseph's College in Darjeeling. He briefly joined a Tibetan guerrilla force at Mustang on the Nepal-Tibet border until this resistance group was destroyed. He studied modern Chinese history in France in 1972, and subsequently served at the China desk of the Tibetan Office of Research and Analysis. Norbu was one of the convenors of the first Tibetan Youth Congress (1970), which is now the largest Tibetan political organization. He is a playwright and author; his books include Illusion and Reality *and* Warriors of Tibet. *Norbu was Director of the Tibetan Institute of Performing Arts (1979-1984). Currently he is one of the founding directors of the Amnye Machen Institute, Tibetan Centre for Advanced Studies in Dharamsala, India.*

LHASANG TSERING

The Issue Is Independence

THE VERY FIRST THING we must understand about independence is that it is not an item of trade in a business deal. The basic motive for business being profit, it is understandable to expect that there would be a change in business if and when there is no profit. The struggle for independence is different. Here the basic motive and purpose being one of justice—of right and wrong—there cannot and must not be any change of purpose merely because there is no profit or personal gain, or even because victory does not seem to be within sight. People of honesty and moral courage do not surrender just causes when faced with obstacles or because they feel they are going to lose.

I am convinced that the only guarantee to the survival of our people, our religion and culture and even our land, is independence. I am quite aware of the achievements of the last three decades and I can see that our culture is alive in exile at the moment. But I believe this is so only because of the hope of returning to a free and independent Tibet. When that hope dies, then the disintegration will begin. Today we stay together only because of the hope that one day, if not we ourselves, then at least our children will return to a free Tibet. When that hope no longer holds true then the bond that has thus far kept us together will be broken and each will go his or her separate way to seek individual well-being. Any hope for the survival of our nation and our culture will be lost.

Apart from the question of justice, there are other reasons why we must not change our goal:

+ It is a matter of practical reasoning that the goal should remain clear and consistent. How can you expect to mobilize the people, the vast majority of whom are beyond your means of communication if the goal keeps changing?

+ Just as a journey cannot take place without one's first deciding on the destination, so also in life one must first want something, a fixed goal, before one can achieve anything. Similarly, for any cause it is a precondition that there be a clear understanding about the goal before there can be any struggle.

◆ Independence is a goal worthy of any amount of suffering and sacrifice. As a people we have already suffered a great deal and I have no doubt in my mind that our people, even for generations to come, will continue to struggle, to suffer and sacrifice so long as independence remains the goal. However, I cannot expect people to make similar sacrifices for a lesser goal. I, for one, cannot struggle to be in association with China.

◆ Looking at it from another point of view, so long as we do not recognize China's rule and so long as our goal remains independence, then China's intrusion into Tibet can be seen as foreign aggression under international law and our struggle will be one of international dimension. But if we change our goal to seeking some form of accommodation within China, then the issue is entirely different. And, as China always claims, ours would be an "internal" affair and we would have no right to seek international involvement and support.

◆ Also, for my generation, to surrender the running of our country and with it the lives of all future generations to China, is like handing over my children to the very people who killed my parents. I know this sounds melodramatic, but the similarity is too strong for me to consider such an option.

Above all, how can we let our fellow Tibetans struggle and suffer and die for independence inside Tibet while we continue a debate here about the goal and purpose of our struggle? How can we justify this to the memory of the more than 1.2 million of our people who laid down their lives in the struggle for independence? And, what will future generations think of us—that this generation, and not the Chinese, were ultimately responsible for the demise of Tibet?

As I write this, I can almost hear the sniveling cries of the critics eager to point out that we must be "realistic" and that we cannot afford to be idealistic because the massive influx of Chinese immigrants into Tibet is reducing our people to an insignificant minority in our own country; that we cannot consider using violence to check this demographic aggression since that would give the Chinese an excuse to use more force to suppress our people and to bring in even more Chinese settlers.

We are at least agreed on one point—that the most immediate threat to our survival is posed by the policy of population transfer. But when I first pointed out this danger in 1980, after returning from a three-and-half month tour of Tibet, no one would even listen to me. Also, it was I, as Acting Editor of the *Tibetan Review* in 1986, who first coined the now much used term "China's Final Solution" in relation to the policy of population transfer. So it is hardly necessary to remind me about this issue.

What I fail to understand is how we can ever hope to halt and reverse this demographic aggression by compromising on independence and accepting some form of association with China. If we accept that we are in some way a "part" of China—does that not provide the legal basis for other Chinese to settle in Tibet? It is true that there are many Chinese settlers in Tibet today and more are entering every day. But so long as we do not recognize the legitimacy of Chinese rule in Tibet and so long as we do not reach some compromise with China, under international law these settlers will be seen as illegal colonists and we shall always have a just and legal basis to call for their withdrawal.

As for giving China an "excuse" to send in more immigrants and to use more force—this can be dismissed by the single argument that China does not need any "excuse." They have many reasons—political, economic and strategic. And, so long as they can, they will always do what they consider to be in their interest to do. Who gave them the "excuse" to invade Tibet in 1949? What "excuse" did they have to devastate our religious and social institutions in the name of "democratic reforms" in the 1950s? And who gave them the "excuse" to massacre our people, to destroy our temples, our monasteries and libraries, to burn our books and to ravage our land? NO ONE! And yet they did all this and more. Why?

It may be correct to say that we should not be idealistic, but it is important that we should not be naive and simplistic either. I have always been of the view that China has no need to sign any agreement with us. Tibet is effec-

tively under their control. No government in the world has
found the courage to question this. And we are not even a
threat to them. What good reason is there to expect that
they will voluntarily surrender to us a part of their control
over Tibet? On occasion they may raise the hope of negotiations. But we must not be deceived by this. They are only
playing for time—knowing that time is on their side. It is
nothing more than a bait to keep us waiting and wishing
for the impossible to happen. And we, not realizing that
time is running out on us, have played into their hands by
concentrating all our time, energy and resources in pre-
senting proposal after proposal for negotiations with
China, as though it is only a matter of getting the right
kind of proposal to bring China to the negotiating table.

To get some idea of the enormity of this problem it is
important to understand that the preoccupation with negotiations with China started in 1978. For fifteen long years,
unknown to the public, the basic efforts of the government
have been in this direction. When we know this, only then
will we begin to understand why people who have written
against this preoccupation or have generally been vocal
in calling only for independence have been treated so
vindictively.

But even if the impossible should happen and China
does agree to sign an agreement with us, what grounds are
there to believe that once His Holiness the Dalai Lama
returns, they will abide by the terms of the agreement?
NONE WHATSOEVER! Our bitter experience has been
that once the immediate purpose has been achieved,
China will not stick to the agreement. What is more, in our

case they will feel no obligation and no accountability to uphold any agreement.

Remember what happened to us in Nepal. To achieve the peaceful surrender of our resistance forces the then government of Nepal made numerous promises. But once our troops surrendered, as a result of a taped message from His Holiness, what did they do? The Commander and some of his immediate staff were ambushed and killed; other top leaders were imprisoned for eight long years. The rest of the troops were humiliated and left to fend for themselves. Why did Nepal behave this way? Not because it was evil but because as an independent country with international recognition and representation and the backing of China, it felt no accountability to a bunch of helpless refugees. I see no reason to believe that a major power such as China will give us a better deal.

Every Tibetan must come to grips with the stark reality that without independence we have no hope. Today our struggle is not only for independence, it is also a struggle for survival—survival as a nation and as a distinct culture. I know there are those who shrink from all political responsibility and involvement by pretending that they are so "objective," so "unbiased," and so "liberated" as to be concerned only with culture—as though the threat to religion and culture has nothing to do with our political problem. Have these people ever stopped to ask why we are in exile? Why our temples and monasteries were destroyed? Why our language and culture were suppressed for so long in our own country? And why cultural preservation has become such an important task for us today?

Regardless of what these people want to believe, the reality is that the root cause of all these problems is the loss of our independence. Without a permanent solution to this political problem there can be no lasting solution to the problem of preserving our culture and national identity. Even our halfhearted experiment at democracy has no meaning unless our goal is the independence of Tibet.

The very fact that we now have a debate on independence—which is to say, we have a debate as to what our goal is or should be—is not only strange and incomprehensible, but painful to me. If we are still not sure about our goal then what have we been doing all these years? Why all the schools, settlements and monasteries? Why do we have a Government-in-exile and why have we been surrendering a part of our hard earned income to support this Administration? If we have no hope and intention of returning to a free and independent Tibet, then why do we continue as stateless people, scattered across the world in a state of constant uncertainty and without the rights and privileges of citizenship anywhere?

Is it because the rich and the powerful have long since secured for themselves and their children the citizenship of other countries while they continue to call on the ordinary people to remain true to the cause? And what cause? The cause of statelessness?

We need to settle the debate about our goal once and for all. But it is not enough merely to bring an end to this debate. We need to realize that it was wrong to have had the debate in the first place. It was wrong on the part of those who drafted the new Charter not to have recognized what is the unalterable goal of the Tibetan people. It was wrong on the part of the new Assembly to have failed to rectify this grave error and to have added to the confusion by raising questions about the goal, then subsequently passing a resolution about independence but again failing to amend the Charter. Our voters must take note of those who did not support independence and make sure that these people never come back to the Assembly.

Though we have no administrative instruments to determine public opinion inside Tibet, for anyone who wishes to see the truth, it is more than obvious that our people inside Tibet long only for independence and wish to have nothing to do with China. In fact, there is no need whatsoever to try to determine their feelings—time and again they have voted for independence with their lives. There is no other more powerful and sure way of expressing one's wishes.

Independence is not only our natural and legal right—it is the express wish of the Tibetan people at large. Accordingly, the entire exile community does not have the mandate to alter the goal of independence, let alone the exile government. And, as for our friends and supporters, while we greatly appreciate their sympathy and support, it is not for them to determine what the goal should be. Voluntary help and support is always gratefully accepted from those who believe in or approve of a cause from a pure motivation. But it is only natural to expect that the goal be determined by those whose lives, future, and very survival are at stake.

Lhasang Tsering was born in Tadun, Tibet. He was a member of the Tibetan resistance force in Mustang, Nepal. Lhasang Tsering was twice the President of the Tibetan Youth Congress (TYC). He helped to develop the TYC into the largest Tibetan group in exile and has been the inspiration for many Tibetan activists. Lhasang Tsering is one of the founding directors of the Amnye Machen Institute, Tibetan Centre for Advanced Studies in Dharamsala, India.

BHUCHUNG K. TSERING

Looking at the Tibetan Struggle

I HAPPEN TO BELONG to what could be termed the transition generation. I was born in Tibet after the country lost her independence and immediately had to flee into exile. My upbringing took place in one of the most trying periods for our community—a period when my parents had to face the trauma of uprootedness and simultaneously having to adapt to a totally alien situation. In a way, my

45

generation seems to be an unfortunate one, having had
neither the pleasure of seeing and experiencing independent Tibet nor the easy upbringing that present-day
Tibetan children have.

Being an Aquarian (this is one of the many assumptions
that I have been forced to make to adapt to modern ways;
like many of the Tibetans of my generation, I do not know
my real birthday) of sort, I often tend to indulge in day-
dreaming. During these occasions, I tend to dwell on our
situation in addition to dreaming of other mundane matters. I try to find answers to such questions as, "What do I
think about the Tibetan struggle? How is it personally rele-
vant to me? What would be my reaction to a free Tibet?"

I may not be wrong in assuming that a majority of the
Tibetans in exile, I mean of the younger generation, may
not have done any deep thinking on the different aspects
of the Tibetan struggle. We have all been brought up in
such a situation which automatically made us a part and
parcel of the Struggle. Right from our childhood days at
home, the moral and political teaching at the schools and
the general atmosphere of the Tibetan community at large
have inculcated in us a sense of patriotism and nationalism. As is the nature of Tibetans, we have taken these
things for granted without any questions. We have got into
what could be called a mind-set. Yes, we do have our
annual ablutions like the March 10 Uprising Day or
Human Rights Day when we mouth slogans. But these
seem to have become more a part of our annual ritual
rather than an occasion for us to think of our fate. We do
not seem to have put our thoughts into daily practice. The

need of the hour is to do a rethinking. Put in Buddhistic
terms, we need to meditate awhile over the nature of our
Struggle.

This is not to reduce the significant role played, and still
being played, by organizations like the Tibetan Youth
Congress. Rather, it is a lamentation of the lack of func-
tional utility of our political thoughts. Ever since its incep-
tion, the Tibetan Youth Congress (TYC) has been making
great contributions in the political awakening of the
Tibetans. The TYC has become a forum for the young
Tibetans to exchange ideas and to voice their feelings on
different aspects of the Tibetan situation. In recent times,
the organization has come to symbolize the unwavering
struggle of the Tibetan people to regain the independence
of Tibet. After the Tibetan government came out with initiatives which planted seeds of confusion in the minds of
the people, it was the TYC which continued to call clearly
for a free Tibet and nothing less.

The eighth general body meeting of the TYC has man-
dated the new TYC central executive members to start the
process of founding a political party. It is the TYC's belief
that if the Tibetan people need to learn the art of govern-
ing ourselves, in preparation for the day when we can
return to Tibet, then the training needs to begin now.
Additionally, with the increased democratization of our
Administration, there is a scope for political parties to play
meaningful roles in the development of our community.
The transition from a leader-oriented Administration to a
people-oriented one is taking place. In order to have a
smooth transition, the input of political parties is neces-

sary. Above all, the TYC's political party will also be able
to undertake such activities which will help the Tibetan
community from getting diverted from the objective of our
struggle.

Having said that, let me get back to the pertinent question of my feelings on the independence of Tibet. I believe
freedom is the birthright of the Tibetan people. There cannot be any concessions on this. Even if, on account of the
exigency of the situation, a solution can be found by set-
tling for something less than independence, this may be
only a temporary one. For, we may then be faced with very
many other problems in such a post-solution situation.
The first problem, I would envisage, would be that we
would not have any guarantee that the Chinese authorities
will stop interfering in our affairs. More specifically, it
becomes a moot point whether such a solution will be able
to halt the influx of Chinese population into the region, an
issue which is of great concern to us at the moment.
Consistency is not a virtue for which the Chinese are
famous. Secondly, we may also be faced with conflicts
similar to the one being faced by certain countries present-
ly, namely interracial feuds.

The question whether the Tibetans in exile will return to
Tibet in the likelihood of a solution is of secondary importance. Even if we assume that many Tibetans in exile may
not wish to return, it does not follow that we should drop
the struggle. I subscribe to the belief that our struggle is
not just for the welfare of this generation of Tibetans
alone. Rather, the struggle is for the basic right of the
Tibetan identity to survive. Put this way, we realize that

this generation of Tibetans do not have the right to give away the freedom struggle merely because it is politically unrealistic and impractical.

The new generation of Tibetans in exile do not know what Tibet looks like and so they do not have the emotional attachment to the country that the older generation has. However, having been brought up in modern societies, the young Tibetans are very conscious of their identity. No matter where they live, they realize the fact that they do not belong to that society. Rather, the feeling of being a Tibetan is automatically strong. Just as our parents were encouraged to continue the struggle by their religious and emotional attachment to Tibet, the young generations are moved to nationalistic and patriotic feelings on account of the importance they place on their identity. Thus, even if we are unable to see the sun of freedom in this generation, we should have the determination to hand over to the coming generation a firm foundation to continue the struggle. We owe it to posterity to see that they, too, are not denied the right to determine their destiny, which is also a part of the struggle being launched by this generation.

The Tibetan Government-in-exile is within its right to probe all avenues for solutions to the Tibetan problem— solutions which the government assumes would be in the interest of the Tibetan masses. Therefore, in recent years, particularly since the establishment of contacts with the Chinese, we have seen a number of initiatives from the Tibetan side. Some of these have even gone to the extent of giving concessions to accommodate Chinese interests. But, unfortunately, we have not seen any serious public debate on these issues within the Tibetan community in exile. (I am stressing the views of the Tibetans in exile because I am conscious of the fact that our brethren inside Tibet do not have the freedom to exercise their free will.)

In the absence of any established think tanks, I believe the different organizations within our community should take the task of educating the public on the pros and cons of the issues. We need to break the taboo of not talking about "inauspicious" matters by putting these under the carpet. Whether the issue is one of the independence of Tibet or of our relationship with Bhutan, we need to let the Tibetan masses know both sides of the issue. Only then will the solutions that we try to find be stable. Before we even decide what sort of future to have, it is important that we discuss it.

Bhuchung K. Tsering was the Public Relations Officer of the Tibetan Youth Congress. Currently he is the editor of Tibetan Bulletin.

CHUKIE SHAKABPA WANGDU

"Keep the Pressure On"

T HE MAY AND JUNE, 1993 protest demonstrations in Lhasa were the most recent of hundreds of expressions of Tibetan rage against China's colonial rule in Tibet. The rage that Tibetans feel is against the illegal occupation of their land, and the pillage, destruction, torture, and killings that followed and continue to this day. But after forty-four years of brutal occupation of Tibet,

China has failed hopelessly in its effort to overpower the national spirit of the Tibetan people. The Tibetan national spirit has been passed down from generation to generation, and it will continue to be passed on like a torch being transferred from one runner's hand to another's in a race against tyranny. What burns deep in the heart of every Tibetan is the belief that we are a distinct people with an over two-thousand-year history, culture and experience. It is this truth that has fueled our struggle for the restoration of our nation's independence these last forty-four years.

Continuing struggles in different parts of the world underscore the fact that when a people's land is occupied by force and there is economic disparity and lack of human rights, then the resolve to right the wrong is deep and relentless. The difference is the Tibetan Freedom Movement is committed to nonviolence, and it is this commitment which has helped us to gain moral support around the world. The question now is not whether China will restore Tibet's independence, but when!

In the postwar world of 1949, when China invaded Tibet, the United States' attention was focused on the war in Korea. India, newly independent and insecure, was looking to China for a strong ally. The survival of Tibet was not in the national interests of those countries who could have helped. So all China had to do was to march in and claim Tibet as her own.

Having failed to overcome the Tibetan national spirit through brute force, and threatened by the momentum of the Tibetan Freedom Movement, China is now embarked on its "final solution" for Tibet—i.e., the total and complete genocide of the Tibetan race. Unless we step up our pressure, China might indeed succeed in her design this time. Under the Population Transfer policy, China has opened up its population floodgates into Tibet, whereby today, more than 7.5 million Chinese are settled in Tibet, making Tibetans a second-class minority in their own land, displaced from their livelihoods and homes, and with little hope for equal education, medical care, and housing. Under the One Child/One Family policy of population control, China has targeted Tibetan women and Tibet's future generation. Forced abortions and forced sterilizations of Tibetan women, and infanticide of newborn Tibetans are rampant in Chinese-run hospitals and clinics in Tibet. This campaign to exterminate a people is reminiscent of Hitler's "final solution" for the Jews.

In the postcold-war world of today, we find democracy breaking down the iron walls of communism, Asia basking in an economic boom, and the United Nations taking a stronger role in maintaining world order. The inexorable advance of high technology together with international educational exchanges have helped to spread democratic ideals, global economy, human rights and freedom around the world, and China cannot remain an outlaw in the world's political arena.

We have witnessed the withdrawal of Soviet troops from Afghanistan, Operation Desert Storm to free Kuwait, the dismantling of the Berlin Wall, the end to apartheid in South Africa, and the dissolution of the Soviet Union into independent, democratic nation-states. Today, the Chinese people are having a taste of free enterprise, tomorrow they will demand political freedom. Democracy is pushing at China's door and the Chinese Communist Party will have to rethink their presence in Tibet. Already, the free world recognizes the Dalai Lama to be the true leader of Tibet and Tibet to be an occupied country.

We need to accelerate our bid to seek the support of newsroom editors, filmmakers, educators, legislators, think tanks, business and grassroots people. The winds of change are now blowing our way, but we must keep the pressure on because China is formidable and full of tricks. Until the Tibetan national flag is seen flying atop the Potala, exiled Tibetans and Tibet support groups must neither rest nor become complacent. We must work, as never before, on all fronts, and take advantage of the resources of high technology to inform the world, especially the Chinese people, about Tibet.

Unlike the China of Mao Tse-tung, today's China is too involved globally not to heed the expressions of concern and disdain by the world public. The changing world will inevitably force China to loosen her stranglehold on Tibet. At that time, if we have done our homework well, we will even have mustered enough moral support among the Chinese themselves to pressure their government to return Tibet to the Tibetans.

Chukie Shakabpa Wangdu heads the Tibetan Women's Association of the New York/New Jersey area. She is an activist for Tibetan independence.

YODEN THONDEN

The Indigenous Route: A Path Not Yet Taken

Y ES, THE ISSUE IS INDEED independence, but in pursuit of this goal we must explore all possible routes. For many years we Tibetans, Tibet support groups, and members of the international community have focused our attention on human rights issues in Tibet, realizing that we garnered far greater support against human rights violations than we did for independence.

This approach has allowed us access to international forums from which we otherwise would have been excluded; it has provided us space in which we have developed a voice in the international community.

In recent years some have argued that the human rights discourse has obscured the true goal of the Tibetan people, the restoration of Tibetan independence. Realizing that the present climate may not be receptive to a direct campaign for outright independence, we should push forth our agenda using all means available until a more opportune time arises. In pursuing alternative routes to independence such as the indigenous route, we may even create the very conditions which would in the end give rise to Tibetan independence. This is not to say that the independence issue should be dropped until a later time; it must be continually pressed forward. But we must also consider that the indigenous route may allow us yet another vehicle for development of the voice for Tibetan independence. It is worth some exploration and thought.

Alternative avenues are particularly appropriate considering the recent signals given by China regarding our hitherto dominant means of redress, human rights. The *White Paper on Human Rights in China*, released in November of 1991, signals China's first attempt to address human rights concerns raised by the international community. Although awkward and incredible in form and substance, the *White Paper* reflects China's recognition of the need to address and defend its record on human rights. The effects are twofold. On the one hand, the Chinese leadership's decision to enter into a dialogue on human rights, whether

intentional or not, has opened the door to change. China's
new involvement in the human rights discourse, if continued, will inevitably lead to the creation and respect for
human rights norms in Tibet and China. On the other
hand this change in tactics may threaten the use of human
rights as a tool for Tibetan independence, for what will be
left when the international community is one day satisfied
with China's record on human rights? With this in mind,
we should consider giving some thought to exploring
"indigenousness" as an additional tool for Tibetan independence.

The definition of an indigenous people is set forth in
International Labour Organization (ILO) Convention 169
which states that indigenous peoples are (1) peoples in
independent countries who are regarded as being indigenous on account of their descent from those who inhabit-
ed the country, or a region to which the country belongs,
at the time of conquest, colonization or the establishment
of present state boundaries, and (2) peoples who retain
some or all of their own social, cultural, economic, or
political institutions. Indigenous peoples themselves reject
this definition and the need for definition in general, argu-
ing that indigenous peoples have the right to determine
their own membership and that to allow the power of
indigenous identification to bodies other than indigenous
peoples themselves is to permit the "defining away" of
indigenous peoples' rights.

The identification of Tibetans as an indigenous people
may be troubling to some, but we should ask ourselves if
Tibet's demand for independence as an occupied nation is

not consistent with our demand as an indigenous people for self-determination—I believe it is. And while it may strike some that our efforts and energy would be better focused in other directions, Tibet may have much to gain from participation in the indigenous framework, particularly through the forum of the Working Group on Indigenous Populations of the UN Sub-Commission on Prevention of Discrimination and Protection of Minorities. Such involvement and alliances may serve us well in the future if/when the concept of indigenous peoples' rights gains wider recognition.

Major developments have been made in the area of indigenous rights in recent years. The primary catalyst for these changes has been the increased activism and vocalism of indigenous peoples themselves. International gatherings of indigenous peoples' organizations rejected national and international policies of integration and assimilation of indigenous peoples, and called for the adoption of new legal standards aimed at the achievement of self-determination.

In 1986, the ILO heeded the demands of indigenous peoples when it decided to revise its convention on indigenous peoples, which was adopted in 1957, to eliminate the convention's paternalistic and integrationist bent and replace it with one that promoted greater autonomy and respect for the right of indigenous peoples to control their own destinies. These revisions were set forth in ILO Convention 169 which was adopted on June 7, 1989.

Convention 169's recognition that indigenous peoples should be allowed to preserve as much of their distinct

social and economic structures as they desire, coupled
with the active role it accords to indigenous peoples in
decisions affecting their lives and lands, all point to the
emergence of a high degree of internal autonomy for
indigenous peoples. The vital issues of external political
autonomy and self-determination, however, were inten-
tionally omitted from Convention 169 out of deference to
the UN body. This was a disappointment for many indigenous peoples. The ILO deliberative bodies expressly stated
that they would make no decision as to whether and to
what degree self-determination attaches to indigenous peoples. Such questions would be better decided in the more
appropriate spheres of the United Nations system where
indeed such deliberations are today taking place in the
Working Group.

The Working Group is currently preparing a Draft
Universal Declaration of the Rights of Indigenous Peoples,
the provisions of which reflect the direct input and influence of indigenous peoples themselves in an unparalleled
manner. The Working Group was formed in 1981 by the
UN Economic and Social Council, largely in response to a
lengthy study on the status of indigenous peoples around
the world undertaken by the UN Sub-Commission. The
Working Group is unique among UN organs in that it
allows oral and written participation from any organization
that wishes to be heard. It holds annual sessions which
are attended regularly by approximately four hundred per-
sons, including representatives from over fifty indigenous
peoples' organizations and observers from over two dozen
national governments. The Working Group thus provides

indigenous peoples with an unprecedented forum for self-expression in the international arena from which we Tibetans could benefit.

The Draft Declaration will ultimately be submitted for ratification by the UN General Assembly. Once adopted, the Declaration will stand as the single most binding legal authority of the international community with regard to the establishment and protection of indigenous peoples' rights.

The Working Group's treatment of the issue of self-determination has been encouraging, considering that the final version must ultimately be voted on by UN member states whose rhetorical sensitivity to the use of the term self-determination and its associated right of secession need not be underscored. It should be noted that the ultimate political status sought by indigenous peoples varies from group to group, reflecting the diversity among indigenous peoples and the circumstances under which they live. For some, complete independence and statehood is the desired status, while for others varying degrees of autonomy or internal self-government may suffice.

While it is clear that indigenous peoples' organizations have repeatedly stated in their own proposed declarations of rights that the right to self-determination is ideologically and politically essential to controlling their destiny, the Working Group's Draft Declaration, in its current form, fails to recognize such a right in the traditional sense. Instead, it guarantees spheres of autonomy in a wide range of areas while retaining the right of the dominant settler state to control external political affairs, similar to the arrangement that His Holiness the Dalai Lama envisioned for Tibet and China in the Strasbourg proposal in 1988. Although this falls short of the independence for which we strive, it is a step in the right direction. We and other indigenous peoples, through participation in the Working Group sessions, should try our best to articulate these rights more fully and in a manner which lends itself easily to external political autonomy. We should attempt to alter the provisions of the Draft Declaration, which is subject to constant deliberation and revision, to effect changes advantageous to our goal of independence.

Additionally, ILO Convention No. 169 and the Working Group's Draft Declaration contain provisions regarding land ownership and land use rights of indigenous peoples, including subsistence rights and land resource rights, which could be useful in addressing immediate concerns regarding Chinese development projects in Tibet which involve exploitation of the Tibetan people's natural resources. These rights extend to subsoil resources as well and guarantee indigenous peoples the right to management and control over any exploration or exploitation of land resources.

Those who are skeptical over the passage of the Working Group's Draft Declaration should consider the following. In the interim before adoption, however long it might be, the Draft Declaration itself will stand as evidence of emergent customary norms which may bring about a convergence of understanding and expectations that are constitutive of customary international law. With this tactical consideration in mind, we should give thought to undertaking an involvement in the indigenous framework. What is common and essential to all indigenous peoples is the right to determine for themselves the degree and manner in which they will exist. We have much to offer to the debate, using our own experiences with occupying China and our visions for the future status of Tibet. We have so much to gain.

Yoden Thonden was born and raised in New York City. She received her B.A. in history and literature from Harvard University in 1989 and her J.D. from New York University School of Law in 1993. She now works with an international. law firm in New York.

TASHI-TOPGYE JAMYANGLING

Independence or Extinction

WHEN WE SPEAK OR WRITE about the plight of our people, we, quite rightly, do so from the point of view of our fellow countrymen in Tibet. That is because their hopes and aspirations are by far more intense than ours. The reason is that they have to live their lives under constant fear of persecution and physical harm—in many cases resulting in deaths. As displaced people in exile, we too have our share of hopes and fears. The following discussion mainly looks at the Tibetan plight from the point of view of a Tibetan living in Canada.

In March 1959, my father's brother was killed on the job guarding Norbu Lingkha, His Holiness the Dalai Lama's summer palace in Lhasa, Tibet, against the Chinese, never to find out that His Holiness the Dalai Lama reached India safely. Thirty-three years later, in 1992, my father passed away in India. He had one simple wish in exile: He wanted to die in the country of his birth that he loved so very much.

A father of four daughters, I am, myself, an old man now. When the time comes, my wish to die in the country of my birth, I fear, would be twice as strong as my father's: I want to die in Tibet for myself and for my father. Right now, however, that time has not come, and I would give my arm and leg if I could spend the rest of my life in a free and independent Tibet.

I frequently wonder what kind of future my daughters (19,16,14 and 11) will have. Will they ever get to go back to a free and independent Tibet, and choose what they want for themselves and for their children? Or will they end up having to live here forever as "Oriental immigrants" of no particular significance ... not even to the Orientals. As I think about our future prospects, I frequently see premonitions: I see grey-haired Tibetan women and pot-bellied-tobacco-chewing Tibetan men precariously doing some form of bastardized "Tibetan" ritual dance—a

Tibetan version of native powwow of sorts—in a desperate effort to cling on to what is left of their identity.

Each time I see or hear about the plight of aboriginals in North America, I cannot help fearing that our people, both in and outside Tibet, could very well face similar predicaments if we do not regain our country's independence before it becomes too late.

Our people are otherwise good-natured, hard working, deeply religious, kind, loyal, extremely responsible, and sensitive to other beings' feelings. Alcohol and substance abuse were almost nonexistent even during the harshest times of our lives in exile. These are our strengths.

I am also pleased to say that Canada is probably the only country on this planet where its citizens are genuinely encouraged by all levels of government to preserve and promote their own ethnic culture and heritage. Even then, the chances of a small group such as ours surviving culturally for many generations down the road is historically nil: From this point of view, we are worse off than animals in the so-called civilized world! The interests of our family cat, Kesang, for example, are well safeguarded from possible harm by the local humane society, animal protection agencies, and advocates of animal rights.

"Is it that bad?" you ask. The answer to that question depends on by which scale you measure the quality of life. We Tibetans tend to measure it by our inner scale. and the reading is dangerously low.

To be truthful, the vast majority of second generation Tibetans in Canada—I am sure this trend, however, is not peculiar only to Canada—can neither speak, nor read and write Tibetan properly. Although extremely patriotic, these young people have very little knowledge of their religion, customs, traditions, and who is who in the Tibetan Government-in-exile in India, and what exactly is being done, and how it's being done! It is true that we are becoming increasingly aware of this problem, and doing everything possible to combat it, but the size of the problem is simply overwhelming. Simply put, it is proving to be too great a challenge to ward off the constant onslaught of outside influences that keep on nullifying our individual family efforts to keep our identity intact. As an "invisibly" visible minority (a mere drop of 500 Tibetans in a sea of 27,000,000 others in Canada), there is a limit to what a small group the size of ours can do to preserve our identity.

Despite all the natural hardships surrounding displaced people like ourselves, until some years back, the quality of my life, measured by my innermost scale, was extremely good. I had everything—a loving family, a most wonderful leader in His Holiness the Dalai Lama, a united and caring community on one hand, and our sacred mission to help regain Tibetan independence on the other. I had a purpose in life, and I used to be proud of my ethnic origin

A loving family I still have, and so have I a most wonderful presence in His Holiness the Dalai Lama. What I ceased to have since is my faith in our current Government-in-exile's ability to work with the people, and stand up for their rights! What is even more depressing is the fact that we are witnessing the beginning of an era of petty politics, and factional squabbles within the Tibetan community which is reminiscent of the sixties!

The head of the Tibetan Cabinet Gyalo Thondup himself has revealed, on several occasions, his belief, that Tibetan independence is not attainable. Coming from a man second only to His Holiness the Dalai Lama, this iconoclastic bombshell is, indeed, not good for public morale. But, if you think this is bad, wait till you hear what the Chinese authorities have to reveal further about this man's beliefs: Yan Ming Fu, Director-in-Chief of the United Front Office of the Central Government of China, in a Memorandum sent to the Tibetan Government-in-exile in October, 1987, had the following to say:

... Since 1979, Mr. Gyalo Thondup has visited Beijing several times. We would like to praise him for the enthusiastic spirit in which he had met with the Central Government. On this visit, Mr. Gyalo Thondup told us many times that he is against making demands for "Tibetan Independence"; that he is opposed to the separation of China and Tibet; and that he is against the instigation of the disturbances in Lhasa. The gist of Mr. Gyalo Thondup's earlier statement is that, based on his ten years' experience, the destination of the so-called Tibetan Independence is unattainable...

You know, Gungthang Akhu Tsultrim was murdered in cold blood in 1972! It is generally believed that the reason was that Tsultrim allegedly received financial help from the government of Taiwan! Our Government-in-exile sent me and the then General Secretary of our Security Office to convey their condolences to the family members, and the followers of late Gungthang Tsultrim. I could never forget the face of the bereaved widow, and the angry air that

almost visibly permeated every part of the colony. Gyalo
Thondup, on the other hand, is elevated to the level
second only to His Holiness the Dalai Lama by the current
members of the Assembly of Tibetan People's Deputies in
Dharamsala!

When not busy electing/reelecting one another, or draft-
ing "Constitutions" and "Charters," or building houses, our
Government-in-exile is very busy working feverishly
towards a "peaceful negotiated settlement of the Tibetan
issue which takes into consideration the welfare of the six
million Tibetans," as the Secretary of the Department of
Information and International Relations in Dharamsala
said, when he addressed the Tibet Conference of the
Americas in Washington, D.C., in January, 1992. "Towards
this end," he continued, "even while in Tibet,
His Holiness the Dalai Lama endeavored for peaceful co-
existence with the Chinese until he was forced to go into
exile in 1959."

I think our Information and International Relations
Secretary summed up what some of us have been trying to
say for quite some time. The bottom line is that our initiatives did not yield dividends, so, why on earth is our Government-in-exile "endeavoring" to repeat something that
has failed not once, not twice, but every single time since
the signing of the so-called 17-Point Agreement with the
Chinese on May 23, 1951? Our Government-in-exile officials will, of course, swear to the effect that they can hear
the sweet sound of one hand clapping. When will they
ever learn that the Tibetan people do not want to show
their left cheek when the right is already blue and black,

and that the people of Tibet do not want another Ngapo Ngawang Jigme "negotiating" yet another 17-Point Agreement? If it seems like deja vu, I think it is!

At the Conference of the North Americas in Washington, I took the opportunity of asking a senior Tibetan government keynote speaker whether or not he makes it absolutely sure, during lobbying activities, that his contacts both in the government and nongovernmental circles know that our principal goal is to regain Tibetan independence.

This was his honest answer from the podium: "Yes," he said. "I always point out to them that we have a political agenda." I guess he wouldn't be a diplomat if he had said no, would he?

Worse still, according to Kalon (minister) Gyalo Thondup's report on his trip to Beijing in August, 1992, it is clearly evident that the kalon had unquestionably bowed down to the Chinese precondition that the Tibetans do not talk of Tibet being anything other than an "inseparable part of the Motherland." The following is an excerpt from Gyalo Thondup's report:

> "...So I stressed reunification (of Amdo and Eastern Kham with the so-called Tibet Autonomous Region) is the minimum requirement because in 1979 when I first met Mr. Deng Xiaoping he told me personally, except for complete independence, everything can be discussed and negotiated..."

The whole world knows that there is no common ground between the Chinese and the Tibetans. Let's "rewind" back to the early 1980s. Isn't it true that every unilaterally created or fantasized "common ground" proposed by the Tibetan leadership, at the expense of our people, was flatly rejected by the Chinese?

Of course it is easier to "lift from the fringes," but the problem lies in the core. When asked for justification for such actions, one is usually bombarded with a litany of politically correct but grossly trite words such as human rights violations, environmental pollution, ecological devastation, and population transfer.

Indeed, human rights violations inside Tibet, and demographic transfers must be stopped. Of course, these are very serious matters that must not go on. What should be done, then? Should we lobby for international pressure against the Chinese policy of population transfers? Of course, we should. Should we do the same thing about human rights violations inside Tibet? Of course, we should. Should we raise the question of environmental and ecological devastation, perpetrated by the Chinese, to the international community?·Of course, we should. But first, and foremost, we must make our bureaucrats understand that unconditional independence is the only lasting solution to the problem whose symptoms, thus far, overshadowed the actual "disease." "Can we regain our country's independence by shouting slogans, and uttering empty words?" some of our bureaucrats have asked before. My answer is that we shall never be any closer to getting what we need by not doing anything about it!

I think it is very important for us Tibetans to be constantly aware of the fact that we are here because the

Chinese are there! Consequently the environment is being polluted, the ecological balance is being disturbed, human rights are being wantonly violated, and the country is being turned into a Chinese colony—all because our country is under their rule! Admittedly, right now we are in a deep hole, and the first thing that we ought to do is stop digging, and start focusing our attention on the real thing that is plaguing our people. If we fail to put our heads together now and revitalize the Tibetan movement, the chances of resuscitating a lifeless political and social carcass, fifteen or twenty years down the road, could be nothing more than wishful thinking! Is that the kind of legacy that our generation of Tibetans is going to leave our children? Don't we owe it to ourselves to get out of this chain of one generation messing up things for the next?

It is a fact that the overwhelming majority of Tibetans in Tibet long to live free and independent lives. Anybody who pays any attention to Tibet knows that. Therefore, by the virtue of our being in the free world, is it not the duty of our Government-in-exile to carry out the wishes of the Tibetan people, and wholeheartedly work for Tibetan independence? I know, it is frequently said that independence is a political hot potato, and that it is not readily salable, expecially when no government recognizes the Tibetan Government-in-exile. If we shy away from these and other political and social discouragements coming from within and outside our community, all our efforts will, in my view, be nothing more than cosmetic.

The average Tibetan is not politically sophisticated, so, most of the time he/she can be led any direction by the

Tibetan Government-in-exile headed by His Holiness the Dalai Lama. If left to think for him/herself, however, the average Tibetan knows that he/she cannot possibly coexist with the Chinese without losing one's life and limb, if you will! The average Tibetan knows that, to come to any form of so-called negotiated settlement with the Chinese, other than unconditional independence, is to submit to the Chinese ways, the Chinese system, and the Chinese values, thus reducing the people of Tibet to nothing more than mere mannequins in Chinese outfits, masquerading as Tibetans up on the roof of the world! Would we want to do that? Would the international community allow this to happen to our people?

The answer to the last question is a resounding "Yes!" The international community has let such things happen to weaker nations in the past, and they will let such things happen again as long as we continue to suffer from weak-in-the-knees syndrome.

As His Holiness the Dalai Lama always says, the final decision, with respect to the future of Tibet, must be made by the Tibetans themselves. The choice is simple: Is it Independence or is it Extinction? My answer is a resounding "Yes" to Tibetan Independence, which His Holiness the Dalai Lama firmly believes is most certainly attainable, and a resounding "No" to efforts that continue to undermine the hopes and dreams of Tibetan people.

My late father once said to me, "Son, you are born once. Therefore, do not die twice." I am not sure that I understand the meaning fully. Whatever it does mean, I am a red-blooded Tibetan, and, given the choice, I would like to live and die like one. So, help me.

Tashi-Topgye Jamyangling is a Tibet activist who resides in Ontario, Canada. He is a former official of the Tibetan Government-in-exile, and was a member of the Dalai Lama's first fact-finding delegation sent to Tibet in 1979.

From Tibet the Cry Is for Rangzen

T HE WORD "RANGZEN" (independence) is the most constant and powerful refrain in nearly all protest documents that have emanated from Tibet in the last few years, whether it be lengthy petitions to the United Nations, humble scraps of paper surreptitiously passed on to tourists, or wall posters hurriedly pasted up in the night (sometimes upside down) on the walls of Lhasa city. In

fact every political demonstration and protest has had as
its essential demand, full independence for Tibet; this followed by demand for human rights, and expressions of
loyalty to the Dalai Lama as the sovereign ruler of Tibet.
Hundreds of such posters, leaflets, pamphlets and mani-
festos have made their way out of Tibet. A representative
few are discussed below.

The most recent of such documents is a copy of a
poster that was pasted up in the center of Rongbo town
(on the wall of the official guest house) in Rikon, Amdo
(Chinghai province). The poster is essentially a caution to
Tibetan people not to believe in the *White Paper* (on
human rights) issued by the Chinese government, and it
assures the people that Tibetan independence will come
soon. It also warns all Chinese to return to China. The
document states that it was issued by the Rikon branch of
the Society for Independence *(Rangzen tsok-chung)* and is
dated August 26, 1992.

A poster dated the first of August 1992, and acquired by
a Swiss/Tibetan visitor to Lhasa last year is a warning to
all Tibetans *"harming the struggle for the rightful cause of
independence."* Interestingly enough, the warning is not
only directed to those collaborating with the Communist
Chinese, but also extended to those in the pay of Taiwan.
Tibetans-in-exile visiting Tibet are also warned against
doing business in sacred images, as also are dealers in
Tibet. The poster concludes on a stern note of warning to
all malefactors: *"We the people know who you are. You are
following a wrong path. You must change your ways.
Otherwise you will soon have to exchange your ill-gotten
money with your life. The nation of Tibet belongs to the*

*Dalai Lama and the Tibetan people.... The Three Regions
(Cholka Soom) Amity Society."*

A nine page petition to the *"leaders of the United
Nations,"* describes the many guises (economic reforms,
etc.) under which Chinese immigration to Tibet takes
place, and also human rights abuses. The petition concludes: *"though the Tibetans at the moment cannot show
their gratitude to the UN, as the nation is under the oppression of the enemy, one day when Tibet gains its independence, the people will surely do so. Jointly from the people of
the three regions of Tibet (Cholka Soom Thunmong) on the
twenty-fifth day of the sixth moon of the Fire Rabbit year."*

Another memorandum dated 4.10.87, from the same
group is addressed to the United States Senate and the
House of Representatives. It thanks the 150 congressper-
sons for sending a message to the Chinese government in
1985, protesting against the oppression of the Tibetan people. It also states that Chinese claims to Tibet are
unfounded and false. The memorandum also noted that
on October 22, 1986, the American Federal Reserve Bank
passed a regulation wherein it was noted that Tibet was an
independent nation. The memorandum observes: *"When
we Tibetan people heard this we became very happy. Our
sun of happiness has risen from the West. Furthermore, the
statement that Tibet is completely independent has been like
food to a starving man and water to a man dying of thirst. It
has made us drunk with joy. From the people of the three
regions (Cholka Soom)."*

A mimeographed list of slogans is dated 10.12.88. The
slogans were probably meant for a demonstration, maybe
the one to commemorate the United Nations Human

Rights Day, which is mentioned at the head of the list. The slogans are uniform in structure, and somewhat Chinese in character with the cry "ten thousand years to..." *(tri-drak)* preceding all the slogans:

> *"Ten thousand years to the historic Tibetan nation*
> *Ten thousand years to the struggle for Tibetan*
> *independence*
> *Ten thousand years to the memory of the Tibetan people*
> *who struggled against China for forty years"*

A very interesting document is the leaflet distributed during a demonstration in Lhasa on 10 December 1988. The first declaration in the leaflet, in Tibetan and English, is unequivocal: "TIBET IS AN INDEPENDENT COUNTRY." This is not only one of the few documents where an English translation is provided, but also one in which the document has been run off a hand-carved woodblock, exactly in the way old Tibetan scriptures were printed.

Jamyang Norbu

Songs of Independence

T
IBETANS HAVE TRADITIONALLY
expressed political dissent and
criticism through song and
verse. Totalitarian control of
Tibetan society has put a halt to this
vehicle of original ideas and opinions—but not entirely successfully.
Even in the bleak sixties and seven-
ties the walls of prison cells have
sometimes seen sad but defiant anti-
Chinese verses scraped on them. Even
toilet walls, especially in Lhasa are
covered with scatological verses and
insults, often directed against the
Communist Party itself. In between
unmentionable obscenities, there is
often a bold **"RANGZEN"** (independence).

The last few years have not only
seen a more open singing of anti-
Chinese songs, but the verses of these
songs now speak outright of rangzen,
where before indirect allusions like

"the sun of happiness" were prevalent. One of the most popular songs in Lhasa, at present, was first heard in 1989 during a religious festival *(Peley ritoe)*, especially observed by women. A rough translation from the Tibetan:

He has not bought India
Nor has he sold Lhasa
The Dalai Lama is not without a place to stay
The Joyous Palace (Tibetan government) is greater
than ever.

I went on a pilgrimage to Dharamsala
The Dalai Lama was sitting on his Golden Throne
On either side Lotus flowers had bloomed
Rangzen will surely come soon.

Another popular song from Lhasa:

Each has to travel his own road
But Tibetan brothers and sisters unite and rise up
Old Tibet was violently stolen by the Chinese
Tibetans are beaten and tortured every day
They eat our food and steal the clothes off our back
By force they stole our Rangzen

Brothers and sisters be vigilant
Look at all the prison camps
Where we are beaten and tortured like beasts
Where we eat a small rotten vegetable with no oil
But even if I have no food at all for a week
I will never forget the Dalai Lama's kindness

Another song in the same style:

Though each has to travel his own road
All Tibetans unite,
Together we will struggle for Rangzen
We cannot make all that is bitter, sweet
Don't listen to them, listen to me
I have a tale to tell
Listen carefully, it is about Tibet
Before our bodies were free
Now our bodies are crushed under the Chinese
Before Tibet was the land of the Dharma
Now it is a Chinese prison
Tibet is full of Chinese barbarians
All our youths are locked up in prison
But even the cruelest torture
Will never alter the courage of our youths
I pray once again for Rangzen

These songs, especially the first, are sung openly not only by Tibetans. Many Chinese beggars and street entertainers have come to Lhasa. Some recite Buddhist mantras in front of the Jokhang. One old mendicant has a little monkey he has taught to prostrate in the Tibetan manner, and it is a great favorite with pilgrims and pious old women. Itinerant Chinese singers and musicians have learned popular Tibetan songs, especially *"He has not bought India, He has not sold Lhasa..."*, which is a favorite of those chang-drinkers who gather at the Naga Temple park (where the Sixth Dalai Lama used to carouse) behind the Potala.

Jamyang Norbu

EDWARD LAZAR

Afterword

S EVERAL YEARS AGO, I attended a meeting with Tibetans and Tibet supporters in Dharamsala, India, which is the site of the Tibetan Government-in-exile. While there, I visited the Tibetan Children's Village, which is a wonderful school and hostel for Tibetan children. I recall looking down at an orphan baby girl in a simple bassinet in their baby room. Her mother had died during a hazardous escape from occupied Tibet over the world's highest mountain passes to the relative safety of India. I think of that red-cheeked baby girl in her bassinet and her mother, and all the other Tibetans who have fled and the Tibetans who still remain in Tibet, some tortured in prison, all being treated as lesser people, and I am troubled by the lack of international response to Tibet. I feel impatient with comfortable Westerners treating Tibet as a fashionable cause but never taking risks and never wanting to be "too political." Not being "too political" has often meant avoiding the central Tibetan issue, which is the issue of independence. This book seeks to rectify the situation and address the central issue of Tibetan independence.

There is no sure answer to how Tibet will achieve independence, but the Tibetan authors of this book point the way. Their essays represent more than words, they represent the integrity of the authors who, in several cases, have worked their entire adult lives for Tibet. One thing is certain—anything is possible if there is belief that Tibetan independence can be won, and little is possible without such belief.

There are many issues to be raised concerning Tibet, such as human rights, the environment, Chinese nuclear testing on the Tibetan plateau, and the population transfer of Chinese into Tibet. But all these issues fall under the core need of confronting the Chinese occupation of Tibet as colonialism and supporting the struggle for Tibetan independence. There has been a call for negotiations between Tibet and China. Prior to any such negotiations, it is crucial that the international community publicly and actively support Tibetan independence. Otherwise, China will be unlikely to respect Tibetan proposals.

Even after forty plus years, Tibetans overwhelmingly reject the Chinese occupation. They persist in their desire to once again have control over their own lives and their own land. Those of us who support Tibet must also persist. In her essay, Tashi Rabgey has written: *"If we have learned one thing, then, it is that our very survival depends upon the achievement of a genuinely free Tibet. The issue, therefore, is independence. Towards this end, our cries will be relentless and our cries will be heard. We will not be silent."* If we listen to these cries with our hearts and minds, we will not rest until Tibetans have regained control of their land and destiny. Hopefully this volume of essays "will be heard."

Edward Lazar has worked in support of the Tibetan people and their cause for several years. He was Co-Director of Humanitas International Human Rights Committee and founder of the Committee of 100 for Tibet.

History and Political Status: A Basic Reading List

The Anguish of Tibet, edited by Petra K. Kelly, Gert Bastian, and Pat Aiello, Parallax Press 1991. (Includes sections on Tibet's role in the world community, human rights, and political initiatives and strategies.)

Tibet Is My Country: The Autobiography of Thubten Jigme Norbu, Director of the Tibetan Cultural Center, Wisdom Publications 1986.

Tibet: The Issue Is Independence, edited by Edward Lazar, Parallax Press 1994. (Tibetans writing in support of independence; introduction by Thubten Jigme Norbu.)

Tibet: An Account of the History, the Religion and the People of Tibet, by Thubten Jigme Norbu and Colin Turnbull, Simon and Schuster 1968.

In Exile from the Land of Snows, John F. Avedon, Vintage Books 1986. ("A noble and eloquent book. Avedon has recreated an entire culture in agony. Indispensable reading." *The Washington Post*)

Tibet: A Political History, Tsepon W.D. Shakabpa, Potala Publications 1984. (The author was the foremost Tibetan historian writing in English.)

Tibet and Its History, Hugh E. Richardson, Shambhala Publications 1962. (The author served for nine years as the head of the British Mission in Lhasa.)

A History of Modern Tibet, 1913-1951: The Demise of the Lamaist State, Melvyn C. Goldstein, University of California Press 1989.

Freedom in Exile: The Autobiography of the Dalai Lama, HarperCollins Publishers 1990.

My Tibet, text by the Dalai Lama, photographs by Galen Rowell, University of California Press 1990. (The Tibetan environment at risk; beautiful photographs of "endangered Tibet.")

Illusion and Reality: Essays on the Tibetan and Chinese Political Scene from 1978 to 1989, Jamyang Norbu, TYC Books, India, 1989. (Compelling essays on the Tibetan situation by one of Tibet's most forthright commentators. Difficult to get but worth the effort.)

The Status of Tibet: History, Rights, and Prospects in International Law, Michael C. van Walt van Praag, Westview Press 1987. (A definitive record of the legal status of Tibet. Discusses self-determination, independence, and the unresolved Sino-Tibetan conflict's relation to Asian politics.)

The Secret War In Tibet, Michel Peissel, Little Brown and Co. 1972. (An overlooked but important book which tells the story of the Khampa resistance to the Chinese invasion and occupation of Tibet, resistance which led to the escape of the Dalai Lama and continued for years afterwards without world attention.)

Seven Years in Tibet, Heinrich Harrer, J.P. Tarcher Inc. 1981. (A good read, and nice Western introduction to the land of snows, originally published in 1953.)

Organizations

For further information concerning
the issue of Tibet and the struggle
for Tibetan independence, contact:

The U.S. Tibet Committee
241 East 32nd Street
New York, NY 10016

Tibetan Cultural Center
Post Office Box 2581
Bloomington, IN 47402

Amnye Machen Institute
McLeod Ganj, 176219
Dharamsala HP India

Office of Tibet
241 East 32nd Street
New York, NY 10016

Canada Tibet Committee
4675 Coolbrook Avenue
Montreal, Quebec H3X 2K7, Canada

Comitè Des 100 Pour Le Tibet (Suisse)
Case Postale 2204i
1211 Geneva 2, Switzerland

Campaign Free Tibet
12 Stoughton Close
Kensington, London S.E. 11
United Kingdom

Bay Area Friends of Tibet
347 Dolores Street, #206
San Francisco, CA 94110

Tibetan Rights Campaign
Post Office Box 31966
Seattle, WA 98103

Committee of 100 for Tibet
Post Office Box 60612
Palo Alto, CA 94306

Los Angeles Friends of Tibet
505 South Beverly Drive,
Suite 924
Beverly Hills, CA 90212

FULL CIRCLE continues its commitment towards creating a peaceful and harmonious world and towards rekindling the joyous, divine nature of the human spirit. We believe in a world of co-operation rather than competition, and publish with the belief that all of us are interconnected.

FULL CIRCLE books are available at all leading bookshops in the country or directly from us. If you are interested in getting books directly, become a member of the World Wisdom Book Club. Please write to us for more details.

FULL CIRCLE PUBLISHING Pvt. Ltd.
18-19 Dilshad Garden,
G.T. Road,
Delhi-110095.